**Mel Bay Presents**

# JAZZ COMPING
## FOR FINGERSTYLE GUITAR
### by Kent Murdick

**A MOVING BASS APPROACH**

# INTRODUCTION

The purpose of *Jazz Comping\* for Fingerstyle Guitar* is to provide a step by step approach for playing both a rhythmic chord comp\* and a bass line at the same time. Situations where this would be useful include voice and guitar, jazz guitar duets, guitar-drums-horn combinations, etc. This bass-chord approach will also serve as a basis for solo guitar arranging (see Chapter 8). The skills taught in this volume are not new and in fact have been used for years by such guitarists as Joe Pass and Bucky Pizzarelli. Unfortunately, until now, the pedagogical material in this area has been severely inadequate.

In order to use this material to it's greatest advantage, you should be able to read music in the first position, know basic music theory, and have at least a folk musician's knowledge of right hand technique. A thorough knowledge of Ronny Lee's book *Jazz Guitar Method Vol. II* (Mel Bay) would be helpful but is not necessary.

Two distinct but interrelated styles are developed in this book. The first is a root-5th type bass line approach which is not unlike (at least in principle) to Bluegrass accompaniment. The second style is an expansion of the first in which an actual quarter note walking bass line is layed down under chords played on the offbeat. Although one style evolves out of the other, both will stand on their own.

I have tried to include enough chords to make the method work but not so many as to create just another cluttered chord dictionary. If you need more chords, I would recommend *Mel Bay's Deluxe Guitar Chord Encyclopedia*. This has virtually hundreds of chords catalogued according to their uses and is perhaps the best organized book of this genre.

\*Comp is short for accompaniment.

© 2008, 1984 BY MEL BAY PUBLICATIONS, INC., PACIFIC, MO 63069.
ALL RIGHTS RESERVED. INTERNATIONAL COPYRIGHT SECURED. B.M.I. MADE AND PRINTED IN U.S.A.
No part of this publication may be reproduced in whole or in part, or stored in a retrieval system, or transmitted in any form or by any means, electronic, mechanical, photocopy, recording, or otherwise, without written permission of the publisher.

Visit us on the Web at www.melbay.com — E-mail us at email@melbay.com

# CHAPTER ONE
# CHORDS WITH THEIR ROOT (OR NAME) ON THE FOURTH STRING
## LEARNING THE FOURTH STRING

Before learning the chords named by the fourth string we must first have a working knowledge of the notes on that string. It has been the author's experience that merely trying to learn a string from bottom to top in alphabetical order is a relatively ineffective method. It is best to learn these notes out of order. Using the left hand fingers indicated and starting on the fifth fret, play and say out loud the letter names of the notes in Example 1. In this and all other examples the Roman numerals represent fret numbers and the Arabic numerals indicate left hand finger numbers.

Example 1

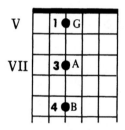

Study very carefully where these notes occur in relation to your fret markings.

Next, starting on the second fret, say and play the notes in Example 2.

Example 2

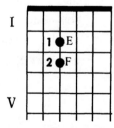

Now combine the two above steps and add the note in Example 3 on the tenth fret. (Think of the tenth fret as being two frets down from the well-marked twelfth fret.)

Example 3

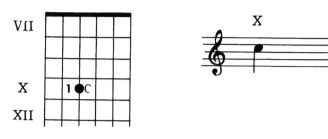

In this final step you should be saying and playing the notes G, A, B, ... E, F, ... C. This will be called the fourth string tune. If you play it and say it several times a day the fourth string will soon be mastered.

Next, play the following random chord progressions using the major seventh (Maj. 7th) chord in Example 4. This chord is named by the fourth string. A simple down stroke strum for each slash mark (/) will be sufficient.

Example 4

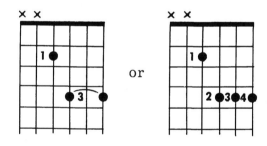

## RANDOM CHORD PROGRESSIONS A AND B

Note: To flat (b) a moveable chord you lower it one fret and to sharp (#) a moveable chord you raise it one fret.

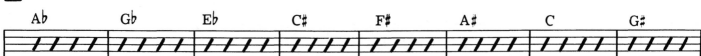

## IMPORTANT

Do not proceed further until you can play these random chord progressions with ease!

# THE MAJOR CHORDS

The following chords have their root or name on the fourth string and their 5th* on the fifth string as indicated by the circle. Notice that there are two sets of major chords, those built up the neck from the root and those built down the neck from this root (Example 5).

Example 5

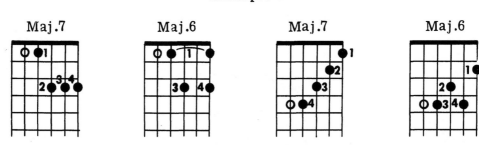

When practicing these chords, use the simple bass-chord rhythm in Example 6. The secret to playing this root fifth style is to let the left hand finger which plays the root, jump back and forth from the 4th string to the 5th string. In cases where a bar is involved in playing the root and 5th (such as in the first major 6th chord) you have a choice of either constantly changing the number of strings barred or starting out with five strings barred. As for the right hand, the bass notes are always played with the thumb and the upper notes with the index, middle, and ring fingers. At this beginning stage we are doing with extended chords what country and bluegrass players do with simple triads.

* At this point you need to know some theory. The 5th of a major chord is the interval of a perfect fifth above the root.

Example 6

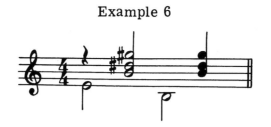

## MINOR CHORDS

Example 7

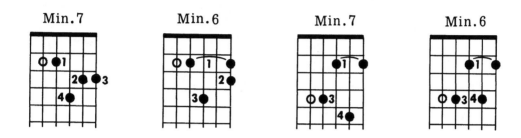

## THE DOMINANT AND DIMINISHED CHORDS

With the diminished 7th chord any note in the chord may actually be called the root or fifth. For the moment, however, we will treat it exactly like other chord forms where the root is on the fourth string and the 5th is on the fifth string.

Example 8

Notice that the 5th of the dim. 7th chord is not directly below the root. This should not cause any trouble since you are not fingering more than four notes at a time.

# CHAPTER TWO
# CHORDS WITH THEIR ROOT (OR NAME) ON THE FIFTH STRING
## LEARNING THE FIFTH STRING

Using the left hand fingers indicated, play and say out loud the letter names of the notes in Example 9.

Example 9

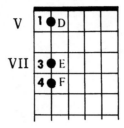

Study very carefully where these notes lie in relation to the fret markings. Next, play and say out loud the notes in Example 10.

Example 10

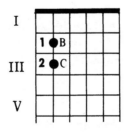

Now combine the two steps and add the note in Example 11 which occurs on the tenth fret.

Example 11

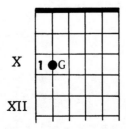

6

In this final step you should be saying and playing the single notes D, E, F,...B, C,...G. We'll call this the fifth string tune and it should be played several times a day along with the fourth string tune.

Play the following two random chord progressions with the Major 7th chord in Example 12. This chord has its root on the fifth string.

Example 12

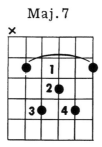

# RANDOM CHORD PREGRESSIONS C & D

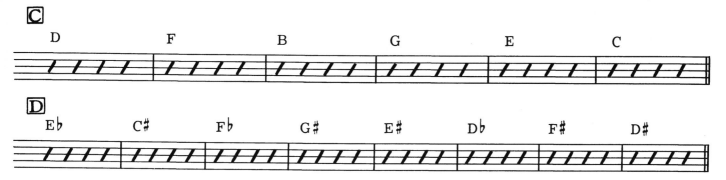

## THE MAJOR CHORDS

The following chords have their root on the fifth string and their 5th on the next lower adjacent string as indicated in the diagram by a circle. Although these chords may be voiced in other ways, I have indicated only those voicings on the fifth through second strings.

Example 13

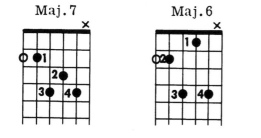 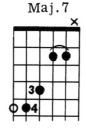 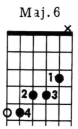

7

# THE MINOR CHORDS

### Example 14

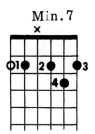 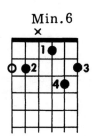 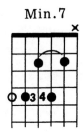 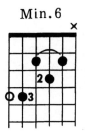

# THE DOMINANT AND DIMINISHED CHORDS

### Example 15

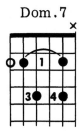 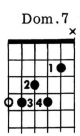 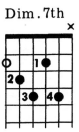

With just the few given chords you now have the ability to play many chord charts. Obviously this mininum number of chords will soon become limiting and you'll want to increase your harmonic vocabulary. More chords and advice on expanding the given chords will appear later in this volume. We will now take up what is perhaps the most important aspect of jazz: the rhythm.

# CHAPTER THREE
# THE RHYTHM
## GENERAL RHYTHMIC DEVICES USED IN JAZZ

Perhaps the most obvious characteristic of jazz that separates it from other forms of music is its deemphasis of the downbeat (beats one and three) and its constant emphasis of the off beat (the &'s of beats one through four). Example 16 is not to be played at this time but is meant to visually illustrate a typical guitar comp over a quarter note bass line (the bass being performed by another player). Although we can never hope to achieve the rhythmic and harmonic freedom of a guitar and bass, we can at least capture enough of the jazz feel to sound convincing.

Example 16

Another important aspect of jazz rhythm is the swung eighth note. This rhythm: 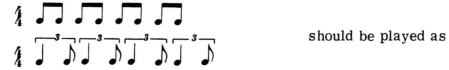 should be played as

It is extremely important to feel the swing beat at all times or your comp will sound more Latin than jazz.

At this point we will go back to the root-5th bass we learned in Chapter One and give it a jazz feel. Example 17 illustrates the syncopated chord over a half note bass line and Example 18 uses the syncopated bass line.

Example 17

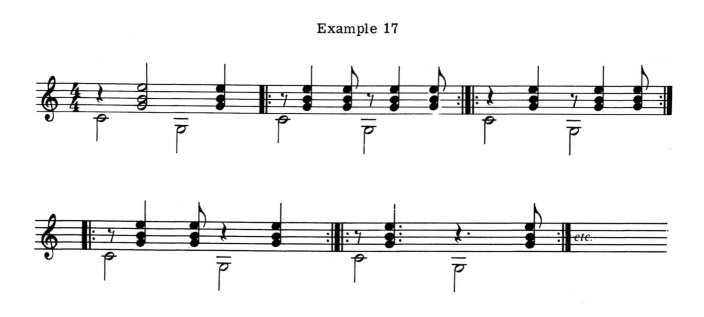

Example 18

We note here that the rhythm of the chords and rests should not be taken literally in terms of duration. The upper chord rhythm only indicates when the chords are to be struck within the framework of four beats and the rests function as spacers to avoid cluttering the score with ties; i.e., chords may be allowed to ring through a rest or terminate before a rest occurs. <u>Since you have already memorized the basic chord forms, the three upper notes in many of the scores will be replaced by stemmed slash marks.</u> For instance, the first two measures of Example 17 could be written like this (Example 19):

Example 19

Examples 20 and 21 should be played using all of the rhythms of Example 17. A chord with an asterisk by it means that you should look to the bottom of the example for a new fingering or voicing.

IMPORTANT  The circled numbers indicate string numbers and the uncircled numbers indicate left hand finger numbers. These numbers next to the root should give you enough information to deduce the proper chord form.

Examples 20 and 21

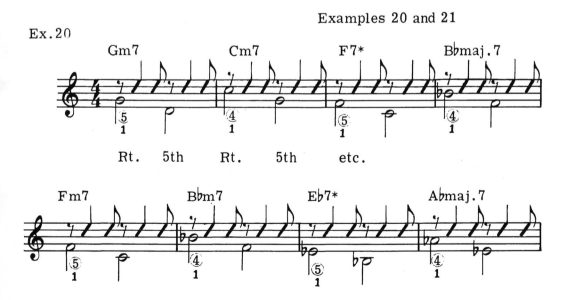

11

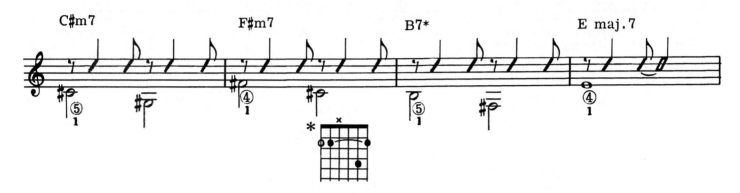

Ex.21

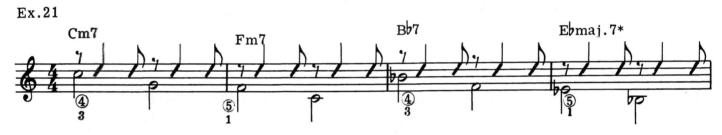

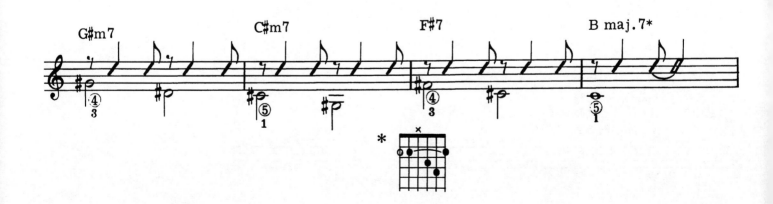

# CHAPTER FOUR
# THE APPROACH TONE

One very effective way to expand the root—5th bass line is to put a bass note, which anticipates or approaches the root of the next chord, on the fourth beat before a chord change. This note is usually a half step (one fret) or a whole step (two frets) above or below the ancitipated root. Example 22 illustrates the half step approach tone (A.T.). The trick to using the A.T. is to start thinking about the next chord root a measure before the chord change.

Example 22

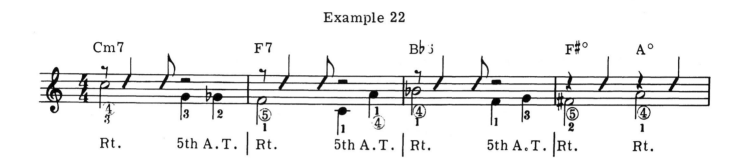

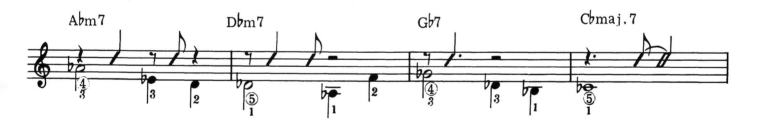

Any chord may be approached from above or below by a half step A.T., but not all chords may be approached by a whole step A.T. Example 23 uses the whole step A.T.

Example 23

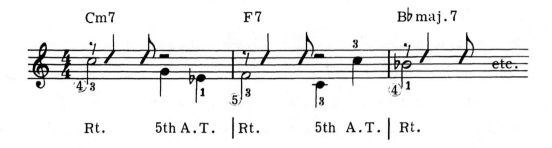

Here are some general rules (that work most of the time) concerning A.T.

1. Any chord can be approached from above or below by a half step A.T.

2. Dominant and minor chords can be approached from above or below by a whole step A.T.

3. Major chords may be approached from above by a whole step A.T. but not from below by a whole step A.T.

4. It is safer to use only a half step A.T. on diminished chords.

5. A whole step A.T. must fit the key of the measure in which it occurs. This is not true of the half step A.T., consequently, the half step A.T. is always the safest bet. Example 24 demonstrates this rule.

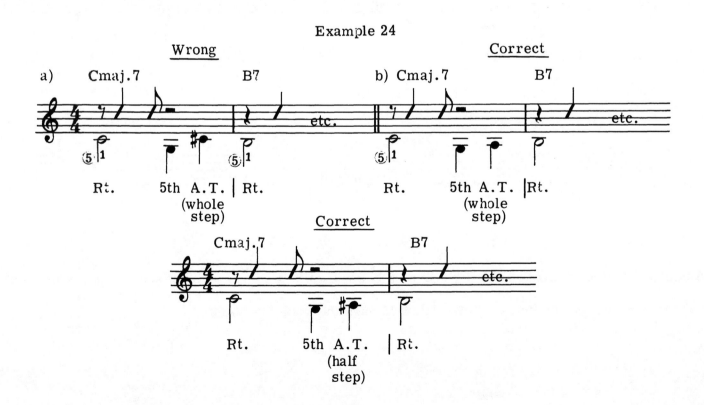

14

To add even more melodic interest, the double A.T. may be used. In this case the entire third and fourth beats are given up to approaching the root of the next chord. A simple way to do this is to fill in the whole step A.T. chromatically as in Example 25.

Example 25

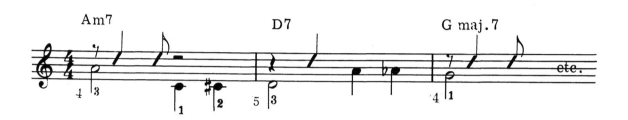

Because the various combinations of double approach tones are so numerous and complex, they don't lend themselves to easily memorized patterns. Therefore, you must rely on experience and theoretical knowledge to gain competence in this area. Below are two more examples.

Example 26

# CHAPTER FIVE
# CHORDS WITH THEIR ROOT ON THE SIXTH STRING

## LEARNING THE SIXTH STRING

Using the left hand fingers indicated, play the notes and say out loud the letter names in Example 27.

Example 27

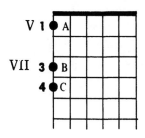

Study very carefully where these notes lie in relation to the fret markings on the neck.

Next, play and say out loud the notes in Example 28.

Example 28

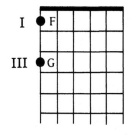

Now combine the above steps and add the note in Example 29 which occurs on the tenth fret.

Example 29

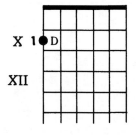

In this final step you should be playing and saying the single notes A, B, C,...F, G,...D. This is called the sixth string tune and it should be practiced along with the other two bass string tunes.

Play the random chord progressions E and F with the major 7th chord in Example 30. This chord is named by the sixth string.

Example 30

Maj.7

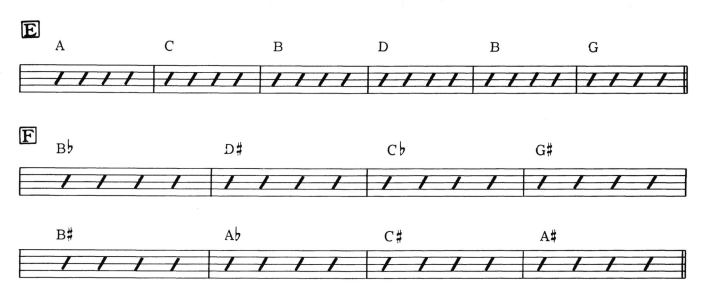

# RANDOM CHORD PROGRESSION E AND F

Ⓔ A    C    B    D    B    G

Ⓕ B♭    D♯    C♭    G♯

B♯    A♭    C♯    A♯

Because there is no seventh string on which to play the 5th of the chord, we must use the fourth or fifth string for this purpose. Unfortunately, this complication eliminates any convenient fingering patterns for the 5th of the chord. For example, the major 7th chord form below provides easy access to the 5th, but when this form is changed to a major 6th, access to the 5th is lost.

Example 31

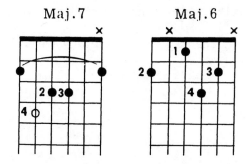

As you learn more chords you will find ways around these problems, but since this volume is not intended to be a chord book, we will avoid complications by introducing fewer chords.

Example 32

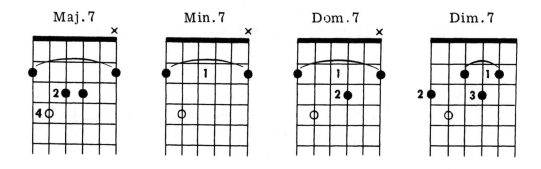

These chords played on the sixth, fourth, third, and second strings. When grabbing these chords you finger only these strings with the right and left hand and then add the 5th (circled note) when needed.

The following piece, <u>Seasons</u>, is based on a chord progression similar to that of the well-known tune <u>Autumn Leaves</u>. It uses all the devices learned so far. Any new chords are marked by an * and the diagrams appear at the end of the piece.

# SEASONS

By Kent Murdick

# CHAPTER SIX
# EXPANDING THE STYLE

## REVOICING CHORDS

As we have already seen, the top three notes of many of the chord forms may be shifted from the inner three strings to the outer three and vice versa. Example 33 illustrates two more instances of this technique.

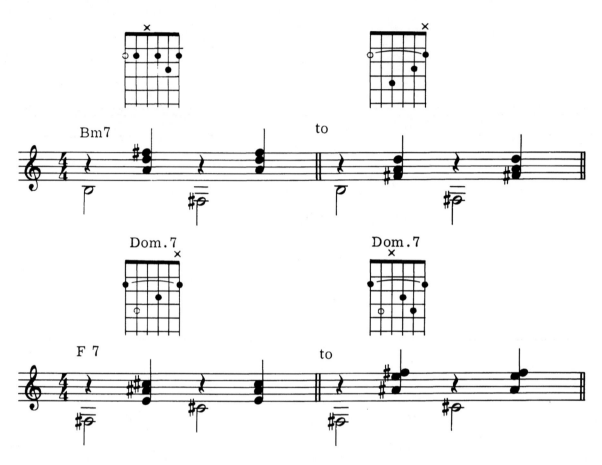

The main concern in voicing is to make sure that the top note, which acts melodically, doesn't jump around too much. Three big melodic leaps in a row can make a chord progression sound disjointed no matter how smooth or well conceived the bass line may be.

## EXTENDED AND ALTERED CHORDS

The given chord forms may be extended and altered in various ways as in Example 34. At this point in your study I would look at the following books published by Mel Bay: Mel Bay's Rhythm Chord System, Mel Bay's Deluxe Encyclopedia of Guitar Chord Progressions, Ronnie Lee's Jazz Guitar, Vol. II., Deluxe Guitar Chord Progressions, Jazz Guitar Etudes, Guitar Finger Board Harmony.

Example 34

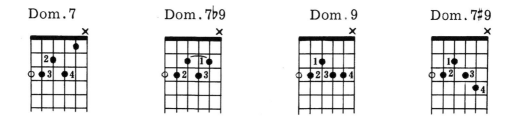

# SUBSTITUTION CHORDS

Substitution chords are very important in forming an interesting bass line. If a progression dwells on one chord too long, the root and the fifth bass line will become monotonous. In this case, we substitute in other chords not only for harmonic interest but to energize the bass line as well. In general we don't want more than one measure of the same chord or more than two chords per measure, and we want to arrange the score so that there is approximately an equal number of one chord and two chord measures. Example 35 illustrates this problem with a solution. (For more on chord substitution see Ronny Lee's Jazz Guitar Vol. II [Mel Bay].)

Example 35

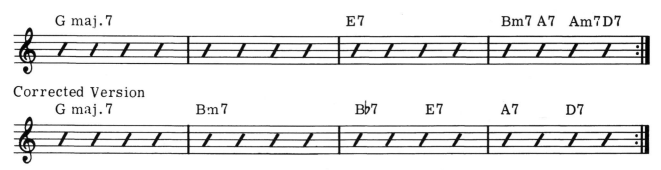

# ALTERNATE CHOICES FOR THE 5TH

Many of the chord forms named by the fifth string have their 5th (of the chord) on the fourth string as well as on the sixth string. By altering the voicings of these chords you end up with two locations for the 5th as shown below.

Example 36

Also another member of the chord may sometimes be used in place of the 5th as in Example 37.

Example 37

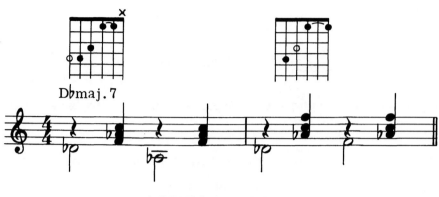

## ARPEGGIATION

Occasional use of arpeggiation, sometimes in conjunction with the elimination of the 5th of the chord can offer variety. An example of this appears below.

Example 38

## FIRST POSITION CHORDS

Most of the standard first position chords may be changed into 7th and/or altered chords as in in the example below. With an A7#5 chord, you probably wouldn't want to put the sharp 5th in the bass. In this case you would either repeat the root or perhaps use the 3rd (C#) for the second bass note.

Example 39

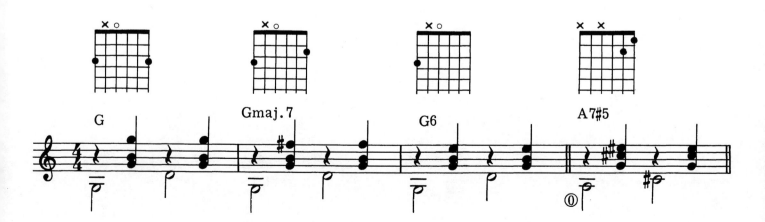

IMPORTANT: First position chords will be used often throughout the rest of this book. Generally the fingering under the root will make it more than obvious when such chords are being used.

## THE MINOR 7♭5 (HALF DIMINISHED 7TH) CHORD

The reason this important chord has not been covered is because it cannot be conveniently derived from each minor 7 form. The minor 7♭5 is used most often as a II chord in minor keys, but it can also occur in major keys as well. The following are three important forms.

Example 40

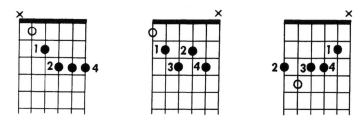

NOTE: In the last chord of Example 40, the left hand fingering must be changed completely when the 5th is used.

## OPEN STRING BASS NOTES

On many electric guitars, first position chords should be avoided because groups of open notes can have an unpleasant timbre. However, open bass notes occurring in the middle of a moving bass line go by so fast as to cause no damage on any type of guitar. The use of open notes is a trick bass players use for making large shifts smoothly. In the root-5th style and the walking bass style (presented in the next chapter) open bass notes are used freely to facilitate shifting and to give the left hand a brief respite from the difficult task of playing two parts at once.

## SEASONS II AND STARS

The next two pieces demonstrate exactly how I would comp on an acoustic (or acoustic electric) guitar. They use all of the above discussed devices.

Stars has a chord progression similar to that of the tune How High the Moon.

# SEASONS II

By Kent Murdick

# STARS

By Kent Murdick

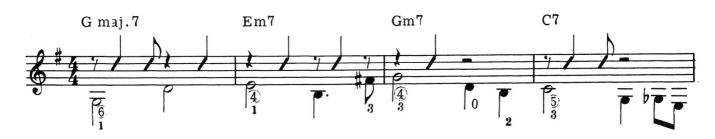

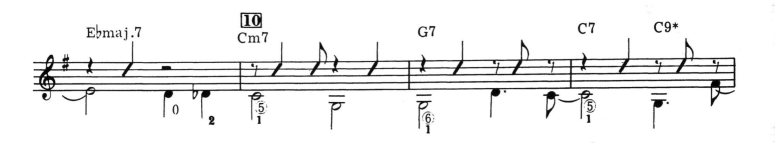

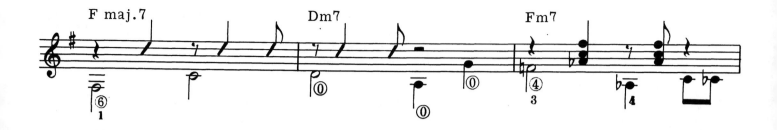
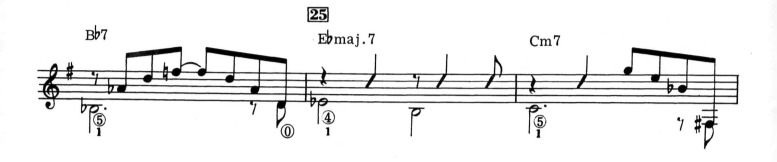

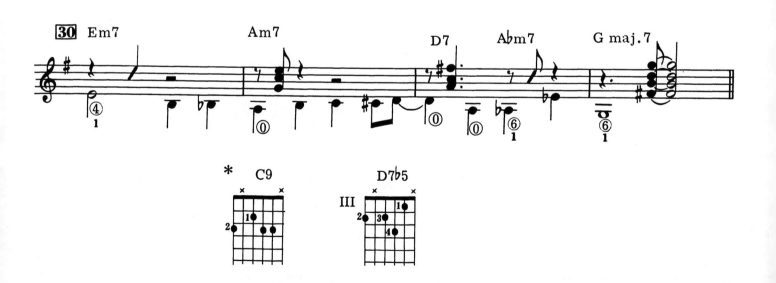

# CHAPTER SEVEN
# THE WALKING BASS STYLE

A walking bass implies at least one bass note per beat or four bass notes per measure in 4/4 time. This is easiest to do if there are two chords per measure. One technique is to use the root and 5th as in Example 41.

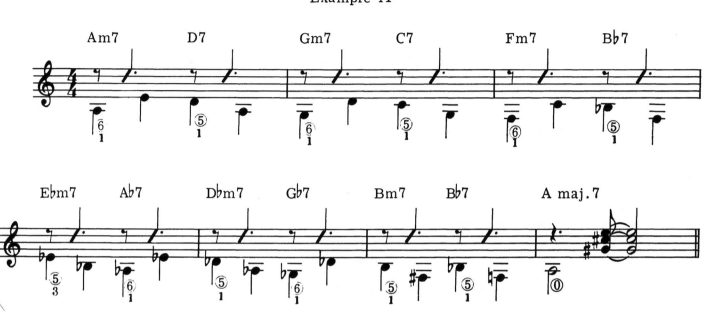

We may also use approach tones on beats 2 and 4 giving us Rt. - A.T. - Rt. - A.T. as in Example 42.

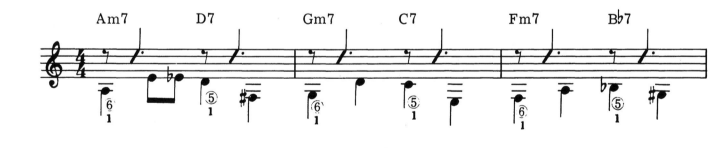

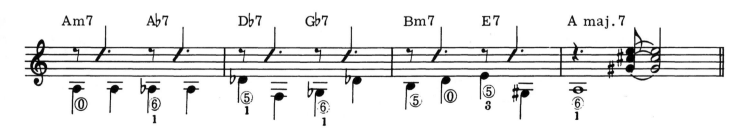

27

Notice in measure four of Example 42 the use of the repeated root. This is a technique that bass players use frequently and is especially useful when the roots of the chords move in a stepwise direction.

Thus far, we have mainly concerned ourselves with the root and 5th while ignoring the 3rd. The 3rd of the chord is very important in walking bass style and it is critical that you be able to locate this note starting from every one of the given chord forms. In many cases you must let go of part or all of the chord form to get to the third. This abrupt silencing of the chord will not detract from the general effect since chords are supposed to be staccattoed in the jazz style. In fact, in some half or whole measures you may decide to have no chord at all. Example 43 shows the location of the 3rd in three chord forms. In the first case, the 3rd is contained in the chord and the right hand thumb merely plucks the fourth string while the chord continues to ring. In the third case, the left hand fingers must jump around quite a bit losing part of the upper chord.

Example 43

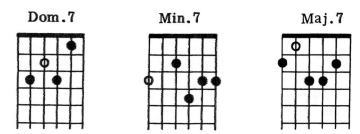

This brings us to the problem of playing a walking bass when there is only one chord per measure. The pattern root-3rd-5th-3rd (1-3-5-3) will not only help you learn the location of the 3rd, but will provide a very strong bass line.

Example 44

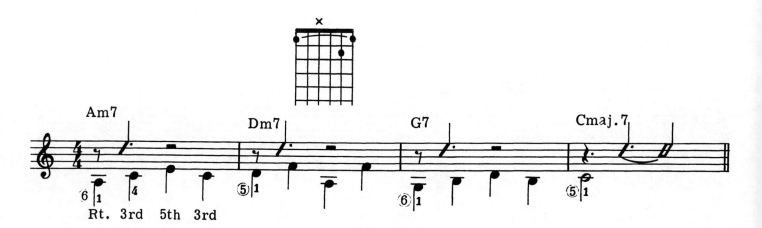

These chord tones may be rearranged to make the line more interesting as in Example 45.

Example 45

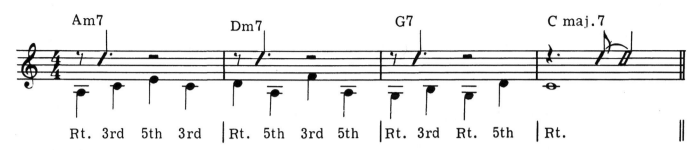

By using the A.T. on the fourth beat we now have enough techniques to improvise a solid walking bass line. The next tune, Mr. Smith, which is based on a chord progression similar to that of Have you Met Miss Jones, demonstrates these techniques.

# MR. SMITH

By Kent Murdick

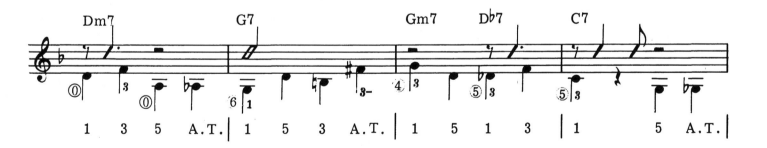

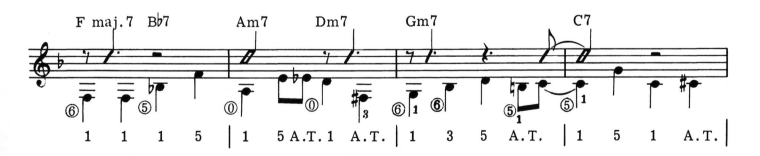

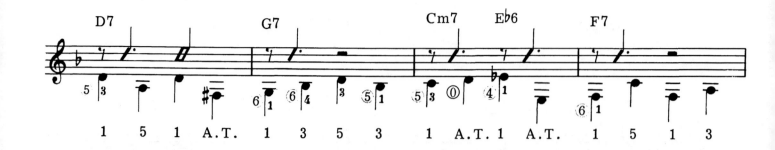

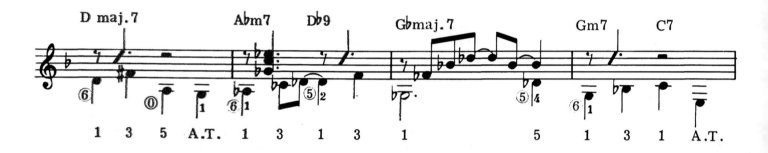
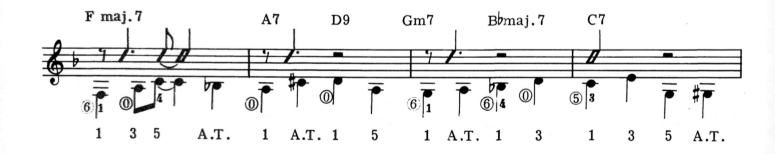
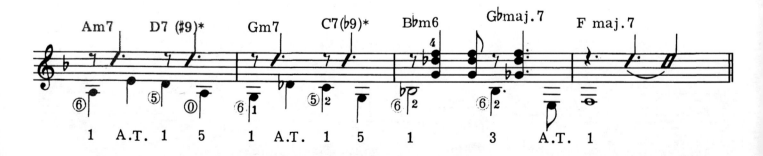

\* Optional altered 9th. you may play just D7 and C7.

The 2nd or 9th of the chord is most often found two frets above the root. A very nice line can be made of root, 2nd, 3rd, A.T. (1,2,3,A.T.) Sometimes it will be necessary to jump down an octave in order to get the 2nd as in measure 2 of Example 46.

Example 46

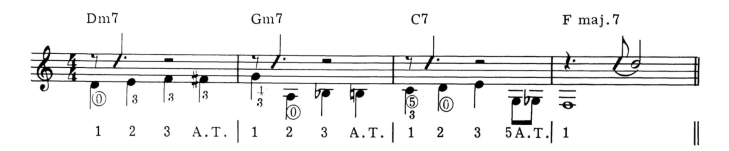

Another cliche is the Root - 7th - 6th - 5th or A.T. (1,7,6,5 or A.T.) line. Note that the 6th and 7th must adhere to the key in which the chords occur.

Example 47

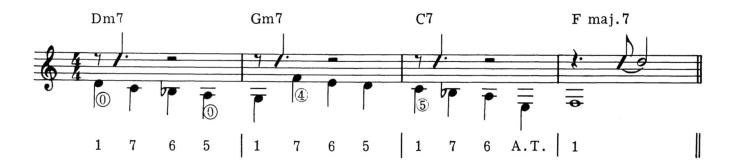

It becomes apparent at this stage that bass patterns do not always translate into easily memorized left hand fingering patterns. To play this style you must become a moderately proficient bass player which includes knowing the notes on the fingerboard and music theory.

Example 48 combines the use of the 2nd and the root-7th-6th patterns, in some different ways.

Example 48

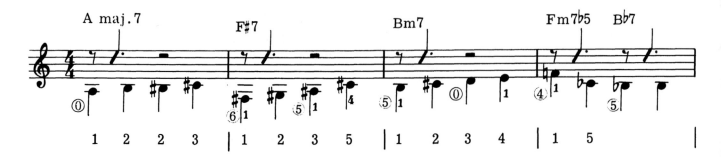

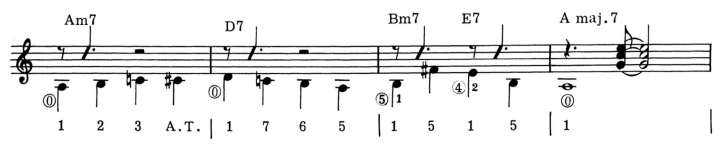

For those who wish to learn more about bass patterns I would recommend Mel Bay's Studio/Stage Band Bass Studies.

The next tune, Theme, has a chord progression similar to that of the tune Georgia. Like Seasons II, it is completely written out.

# THEME

**By Kent Murdick**

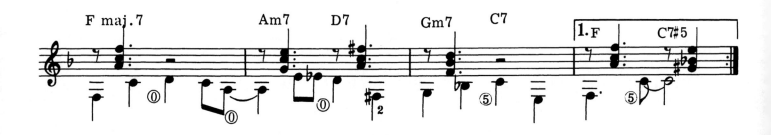

Chorus

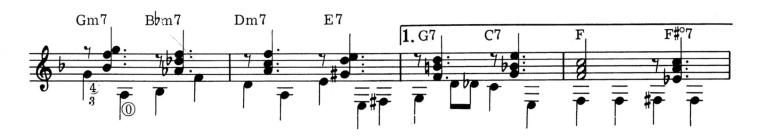
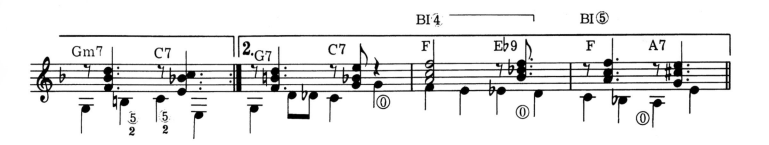
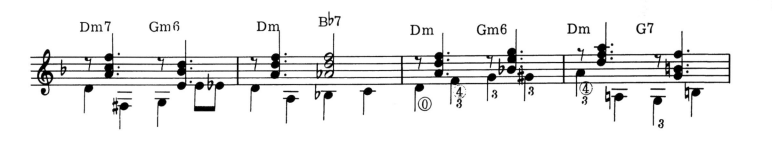

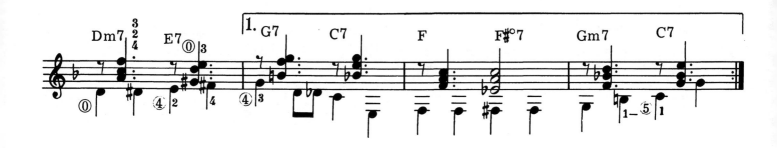
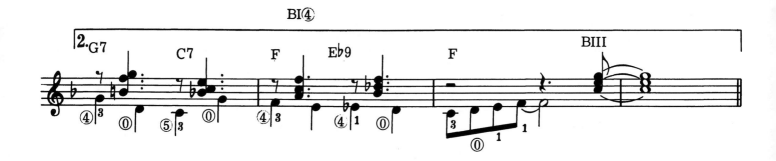

The last tune of Chapter Seven is called Mystique and has a chord progression similar to the song Misty.

# MYSTIQUE

By Kent Murdick

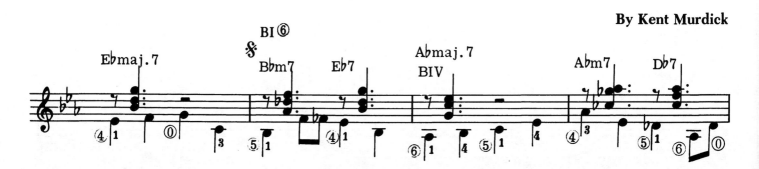

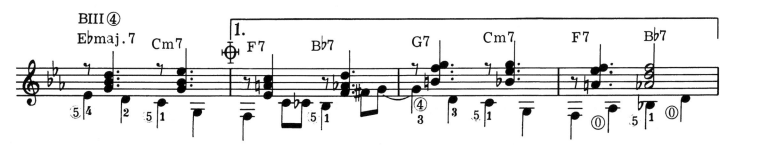

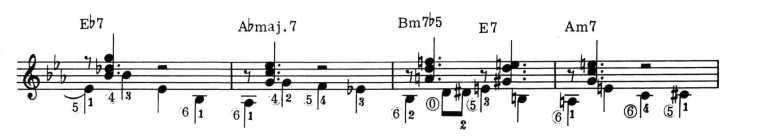
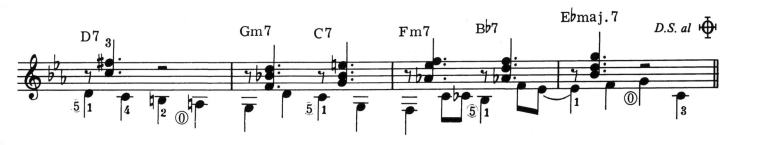
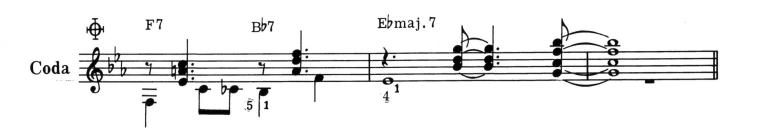

# CHAPTER EIGHT
# SOLO ARRANGING

Although a thorough treatment of solo guitar arranging is certainly beyond the scope of this book, I think a few brief words concerning this topic will be of help to the aspiring solo player. The observant student will probably already have noticed how naturally bass chord comping styles lead to solo arranging.

One of the biggest problems that most solo guitarists have is understanding the guitar's relative strengths and weaknesses, i.e., its uniqueness. The guitar is too often thought of as a miniature version of the piano and hence guitar solos are many times loaded down with awkward phrases. Players are often afraid to rely on the guitar's beautiful tone to carry a line through. Realistically, we must admit that we cannot imitate the voice movement or voicing spread of the piano. But (and herein lies the key) we don't have to. We can keep our arrangements simple from the standpoint of voice movement without losing richness of sound. Remember, simplicity does not preclude creativity.

A very effective solo guitar style can be based on the root-5th and walking bass comping styles. This will be a polyphonic style with three independent parts. The top line which is the melody can move with absolute independence in terms of rhythm and pitch. The bass line moves just like the bass lines in the preceeding chapters, i.e., with limited melodic and rhythmic interest. The inner chord which was previously assigned to the three top notes in the comping style will usually (but not always) be reduced in number and have rhythmic independence.

The above rules are generalizations only. For instance, it can be nice to occasionally put the melody in the bass or to let the inner chord contain some melodic interest. Also you can simplify. There's nothing wrong with playing a measure or even two of single notes. This allows the listener to hear how beautiful the guitar can sound. A good rule of thumb is that you should simplify a little more than you complicate.

The last tune in the book is an original entitled <u>Scotty's Bounce</u>. It first appears in lead sheet form with a root-5th comp underneath. The second rendering is a guitar solo based on the previous comping ideas. A good exercise would be to use this solo as a basis for writing another one with your own bass line and comping rhythm.

# SCOTTY'S BOUNCE
## (FOR SCOTT MURDICK)

By Kent Murdick

# SCOTTY'S BOUNCE
## (SOLO)
(For Scott Murdick)

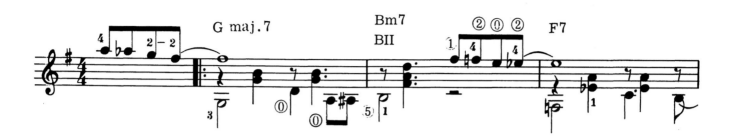
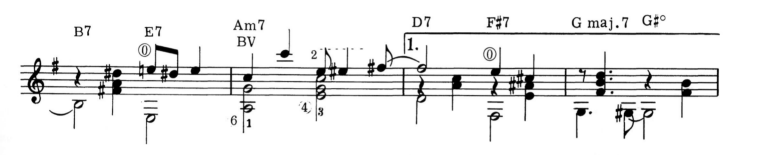
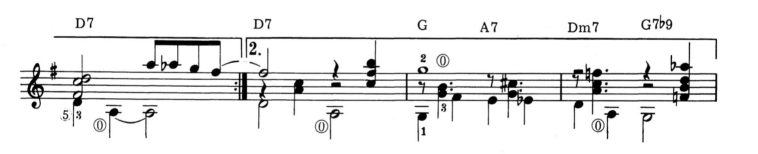
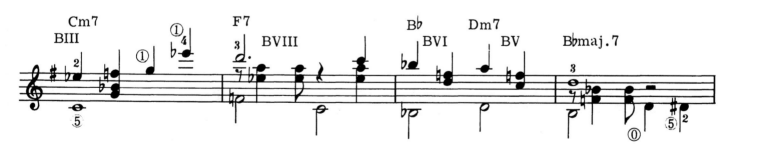

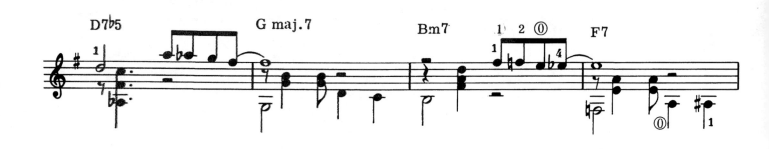
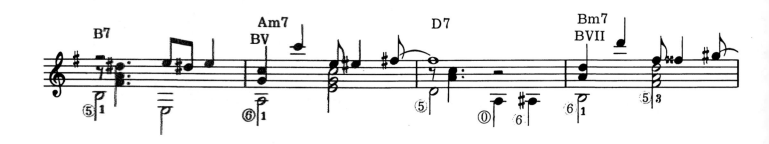
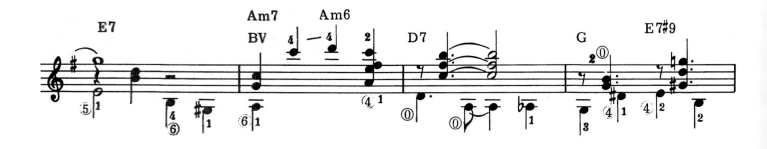
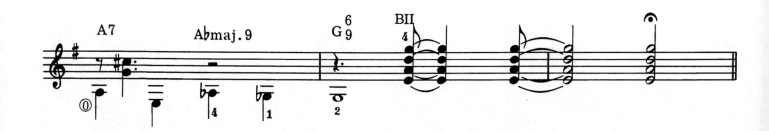